A New True Book

ZIMBABWE

By Karen Jacobsen

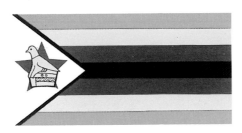

Flag of Zimbabwe

CHILDRENS PRESS®
CHICAGO

Tree-lined Samora Machel Avenue
in the city of Harare

PHOTO CREDITS

© Cameramann International, Ltd.—Cover, Cover Inset, 8, 15 (left), 33 (left), 36 (left), 39 (right), 43 (right), 44, 45

Reprinted with permission of *The New Book of Knowledge*, 1989 edition, © Grolier Inc.—9

H. Armstrong Roberts—15 (inset)

Historical Pictures Service, Chicago—20, 21 (2 photos), 22, 25

© Jason Lauré—7 (right), 39 (left), 43 (left)

Nawrocki Stock Photo—© Jason Lauré, 14 (right), 27, 31, 35 (left), 40

North Wind Picture Archives—18

Photri—2, 4 (top), 10

Root Resources—© Kenneth W. Fink, 14 (left); © Ted Farrington, 41 (right); © Charles G. Summers, Jr./Colorado Nature Photographic Studio, 41 (left)

Shostal Associates/SuperStock International, Inc.—4 (bottom), 11, 17, 33 (right)

SuperStock International, Inc.—© J.N. Ruddiman, 7 (left)

TSW/CLICK-Chicago—36 (right)

UPI/Bettmann Newsphotos—29

Valan—© Christine Osborne, 12, 35 (right)

Cover—Lake Kariba on the Zambezi River

Cover Inset—Samora Machel Avenue

Library of Congress Cataloging-in-Publication Data

Jacobsen, Karen.
  Zimbabwe / by Karen Jacobsen.
    p.   cm. — (A New true book)
  Includes index.
  Summary: Introduces the geography, history, people, and culture of Zimbabwe.
  IBSN 0-516-01110-3
  1. Zimbabwe—Juvenile literature.
[1. Zimbabwe.]   I. Title.
DT2889.J33 1990   90-2202
968.91—dc20   CIP
                                    AC

TABLE OF CONTENTS

The ruins of Great Zimbabwe. The stone tower (right) is 29 feet high. No one knows what its purpose was.

4

THE REPUBLIC OF ZIMBABWE

Long ago in southeastern Africa, the Mashona people built a stone city called Great Zimbabwe. Parts of that city are still standing. Its thick walls are thirty feet high. They surround a stone tower and the ruins of many stone buildings.

Today, the Republic of Zimbabwe is named after this ancient city. Zimbabwe became a republic in 1980. The people elect a president and a Parliament. The people in Parliament elect a prime minister to govern the country.

Almost ten million people live in Zimbabwe. About eight million are Mashona people. Nearly two million are Matabele people. There are almost ninety thousand

Matebele in traditional costumes (left). Matabele city dwellers wear shirts with a political message (right).

people whose ancestors
were settlers who came from
England or other European
countries. Also, more than
ten thousand people whose
ancestors came from Asia
live in Zimbabwe.

English is the country's

7

official language. But many people speak other languages at home. Most Africans speak the language of the Mashona or the Matabele. Harare, formerly called Salisbury, is the capital of Zimbabwe.

Harare, the capital of Zimbabwe, is a modern city.

THE LAND

Zimbabwe is a tropical country in southeastern Africa. It stretches more than 500 miles from north to south. It is more than 400 miles from east to west.

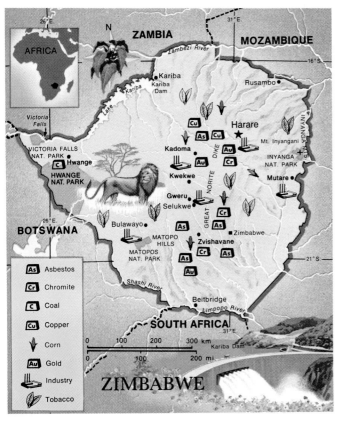

On a map, the outline of Zimbabwe looks somewhat like a circle. Along the circle's northern rim are Victoria Falls, Lake Kariba, and the Zambezi River.

The Victoria Falls, on the Zambezi River, are a mile wide.

On the circle's southern rim is the Limpopo River. The Limpopo divides Zimbabwe from South Africa.

The Middle Veld. The Inyanga Mountains are in the background.

The Inyanga Mountains form part of the circle's eastern rim.

Most of Zimbabwe is a plateau, rising from 3,000 to 5,000 feet above sea level. The highest part, called the High Veld, is in the center. The country's cities and best

Zimbabwe has enough good farmland to be self-sufficient in agriculture.

farmland are on the High Veld.

On both sides of the High Veld there is lower plateau land called the Middle Veld. The Middle Veld is good for raising cattle.

Along the river valleys are the Low Veld lands. People

do not live in the Low Veld because it is very hot and humid.

Zimbabwe lies south of the equator in the earth's Southern Hemisphere. Its seasons are the reverse of those of the Northern Hemisphere countries.

Since Zimbabwe is near the equator, we would expect it to be hot all year round. But because of its high plateaus, Zimbabwe's temperatures are cooler. Only its summers are hot.

PLANTS AND ANIMALS

Zimbabwe is covered with
grasses. It has many tropical
trees such as the baobab,
the thorn tree, and the mopani.
Its flowers include the
hibiscus and the flame lily.
Many kinds of wild animals,

A baobab tree (left) and
a hibiscus blossom (below)

Elephants and cheetahs (inset) live in Hwange National Park.

from aardvarks to zebras, live
in Zimbabwe. In Hwange
National Park, visitors can
see lions, leopards, cheetahs,
hyenas, foxes, elephants,
antelopes, giraffes, gorillas,
and hippopotamuses.   15

EARLY HISTORY

People have been living on this land for many thousands of years.

Sometime after A.D. 800, the Mashona people came. They planted crops and worked iron.

About A.D. 1000, they began to build Great Zimbabwe. Four hundred years later, the city was the capital of their empire. By the late 1400s, people had moved away from Great

The builders of Great Zimbabwe were very skillful. They used no mortar to hold their amazing city together.

Zimbabwe. There were better fields and forests in other parts of the empire.

In 1513, explorers from Portugal came. They were looking for gold and other riches. The Portguese tried to take control of the Mashona's land. But the

Mashona were led by Dombo. His warriors had firearms and drove the Portuguese away.

Later, the Portuguese returned. They brought settlers and Christian missionaries. In 1630 they even chose a man to be king of the Mashona.

The Portuguese made slaves of the east African peoples.

MZILIKAZI
AND THE MATABELE

Mzilikazi was a general in the army of Shaka, the great Zulu warrior king. In 1836, Mzilikazi led the Matabele people away from Shaka's control. They moved north, crossed the Limpopo River, and settled on the High Veld near the Matopo Hills. Mzilikazi's army had better weapons. The Matabele people took over the lands and cattle of the Mashona.

Lobengula, king of the Matabele

The Mashona were forced to work for the Matabele.

In 1870, Mzilikazi died, and Lobengula became king. He ruled over a kingdom that stretched from the Limpopo River to Lake Victoria. The Matabele tried to keep the Europeans out of their land. But the English and other Europeans kept coming.

SOUTHERN RHODESIA

In the 1850s, David Livingstone, a Scottish missionary, explored the Zambezi River and central Africa. Livingstone was not interested in taking over the land. He wanted to end the slave trade in Africa.

David Livingstone and the boat he used for his explorations on the Zambezi River

Later, Cecil Rhodes, a powerful Englishman in southern Africa, became interested in the land. In 1888, Rhodes made an agreement with Lobengula. The African king gave Rhodes the right to look for minerals in his kingdom. Soon, Rhodes sent white settlers and police into the area. They built a town and called it Fort Salisbury.

The whites built more forts and took more land from the Africans. The settlers built houses and planted crops.

The Matabele were forced to move onto "reserves." The reserves were lands with poor soil and bad water. The settlers made the Matabele work on white farms.

By 1893, Rhodes' British South Africa Company (BSAC) occupied most of the region. By 1895, the area was known as Southern Rhodesia.

The Matabele and the Mashona were angry about losing their land and their freedom. For the next eighty years, the white minority ruled the country. But they always had to be on guard against the black majority.

BRITISH RULE

In 1923, Southern Rhodesia became a part of the British Empire. Both white people and black people became British subjects and had to obey British laws.

The railroad was essential in the development of the interior of Africa.

In 1930, the whites passed a law dividing the land between the whites and the Africans. The whites took the mining and industrial areas and all the roads and railroads. The Africans got the poor land on the reserves. The law said the Africans could not go onto white land except to work for whites.

The British government tried to make the white minority give more rights to

Prime Minister
Ian Smith

the black majority. But the whites refused.

In 1964, Ian Smith was elected prime minister of Southern Rhodesia. A year later, Smith's government declared independence from Britain. The country's name was changed to Rhodesia.

ZIMBABWE – RHODESIA

In the 1970s, many black African groups wanted to make changes in Rhodesia. Some groups were peaceful, but others were violent. In 1976, the country was fully involved in a civil war. Thousands of white people left the country to escape the fighting. The black revolutionary armies won victories and grew stronger.

Finally, in 1978, Prime Minister Smith and the white minority agreed to make

Bishop Abel Muzorewa, Ian Smith, Jeremiah Chirau, and the Reverend Ndabaningi Sithole (seated, left to right) sign the document ending white rule in Rhodesia in 1978.

peace. They met with Abel Muzorewa and other black leaders to talk about sharing power with the black majority.

In 1979, the first black majority government was elected and Rhodesia's name was changed to Zimbabwe-Rhodesia.

In late 1979, the new government and the Patriotic Front (the largest rebel group) signed a peace agreement. The fighting would stop and, in return, there would be another election in February 1980. All of the people, black and white, would elect a new Parliament. Eighty members would be black Africans and twenty would be whites.

The political party of Robert Mugabe, a leader of

President
Robert Mugabe

the Patriotic Front, won the
election. The nation was
renamed Zimbabwe. There
was no more Rhodesia and
no more white-minority
control.

RECENT EVENTS

Since 1980, there has been much trouble between the Mashona majority and the Matabele minority. In 1982, Prime Minister Mugabe, a Mashona, dismissed Joshua Nkomo, a Matabele, from his high position in government. Mugabe said Nkomo was plotting a revolution. Nkomo said that Mugabe was trying to do away with Matabele rights.

Harare (left) is an important business city. Bulawayo (right), the country's second largest city, is an industrial center.

In spite of this trouble, Zimbabwe has many strengths. Its farms produce more than enough food. Its industries make other products for the nation.

Harare is the nation's government and business center.

LIFE IN ZIMBABWE

Today, in Zimbabwe, most
of the white people own
businesses in the city or
large farms out in the country.
They live in comfortable
homes and employ servants.
They have modern cars
and many other luxuries.

Many black people now
live in or near Zimbabwe's
cities. The well-educated
blacks have jobs in business
or government. They live in

White Zimbabweans usually have much finer housing (left) than the blacks (right).

apartments or single-family houses.

Other black people come to the cities to find work. They have little or no money. Many cannot speak English when they arrive. They are unskilled and can get only low-paying jobs.

The village women raise corn, beans, and fruits and vegetables in nearby fields. The men and boys hunt and raise cattle or goats.

Most black people in Zimbabwe live in tribal villages, far away from cities. Their houses are made of mud and have grass roofs.

A favorite food is corn pudding, called mealies. It is made from ground corn mixed with water or milk and then cooked. People in

Zimbabwe also like meat stews, served hot and spicy.

Many black men go to work in mines or on large farms far away from their villages. They send money home to their families and return for visits on weekends or holidays.

Many people in Zimbabwe are Christians. But most of the people pray to ancestors or to nature spirits—the sun, rivers, rocks, snakes, lions, and other animals.

EDUCATION

Before 1980, schools in Zimbabwe were segregated. Only white children could attend public schools.

Many black children went to schools that were run by missionaries. Good students received scholarships to attend black high schools. Very few went on to study at universities.

Today, segregation is against the law. All children, black and white, attend free elementary schools together.

A farm school meets in a field (left). In Zimbabwe, public schools are fully integrated (right).

They all study English and the languages of both the Mashona and the Matabele.

There are not enough school buildings, books, or teachers in Zimbabwe. Many children in remote villages still do not have a school to attend.

Lawn bowling was introduced by the English.

SPORTS AND RECREATION

English settlers brought English sports, such as lawn bowling, cricket, and rugby, to Zimbabwe. Some Africans play these sports, but soccer is their favorite sport. Boxing is also popular.

Giraffes (left) and rhinoceroses (right) are wild animals that live in Zimbabwe.

Because there are so many wild animals in Zimbabwe, hunting is an important sport. Foreign hunters come from all over the world to kill animals in Zimbabwe. In remote African villages, hunting is still a necessary part of life.

In Zimbabwe, people observe the Christian holidays, especially Christmas and Easter. Other special holidays are Independence Day on April 8, May Day on May 1, and Africa Day on May 25. On these days there are parades and speeches followed by parties and dancing.

Long ago, in Great Zimbabwe, artists carved stone sculptures of birds. The birds decorated the tops

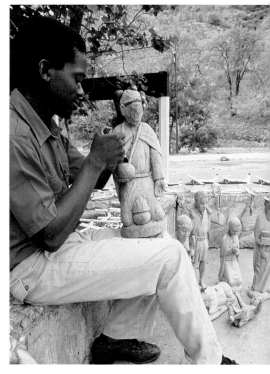

A Zimbabwean Christmas celebration (above). A wood carver at work (right).

of the city's buildings and walls. Some of those stone birds can be seen in a museum in Masvingo. Today, artists in Zimbabwe carve stone, wood, and ivory sculptures.

The music of Zimbabwe is popular around the world.

43

A performance by a school band and dancers

The music is called *jit* and has a happy rhythm for dancing.

Today, in Zimbabwe, the people run their own government, and they are learning to get along with each other. Their cities are busy, modern, and growing.

Yet, in many places, the land
is unchanged. It is still wild
and very beautiful. The people
of Zimbabwe have much to
enjoy in their wonderful, wonder-
filled country.

WORDS YOU SHOULD KNOW

aardvark (ARD • vark) — a burrowing mammal with a long snout that feeds on ants and termites

ancestor (AN • sess • ter) — a grandparent or forebear earlier in history

baobab (BAH • o • bob) — a tall tree with a thick trunk and fruit that can be eaten

civil war (SIH • vil WAHR) — a war between two groups in the same country

explorer (ex • PLOHR • er) — a person who travels to an unknown land to find out what is there

hibiscus (hie • BISS • kus) — a woody plant with large red, pink, or white flowers

humid (HYOO • mid) — damp, moist

industrial (in • DUSS • tree • al) — having many factories and business places

majority (mah • JOR • ih • tee) — the greater number or part

Mashona (mah • SHOW • na) — a group of people who have lived in Zimbabwe for many centuries

Matabele (mah • tah • BEL • lay) — a group of people who entered Zimbabwe in the nineteenth century and defeated the Mashona

mealies (MEE • leez) — corn pudding

minority (my • NOR • ih • tee) — the smaller number or part

missionary (MISH • un • airy) — a person who travels to another country to bring a certain religion to the people there

mopani (mo • PAH • nee) — a tree with very hard wood

Parliament (PARL • ah • mint) — the lawmaking body of some governments

plateau (plat • OH) — high, flat land

reserves (rih •ZERVZ) — lands set aside for certain groups of people

scholarship (SKAH •ler •ship) — an award of tuition payments to attend a school

segregation (sehg •rih •GAY •shun) — the separating of people on the basis of race, religion, or some other factor

subjects (SUB •jekts) — people who are subject to a government; citizens

tropical (TRAH •pih •kil) — having to do with the parts of the earth just to the north and south of the equator

veld (VEHLD) — a grassland, usually with scattered trees or shrubs

INDEX

About the Author

Karen Jacobsen is a graduate of the University of Connecticut and Syracuse University. She has been a teacher and is a writer. She likes to find out about interesting subjects and then write about them.